PULP SPEED FOR PROFESSIONAL WRITERS

BUSINESS FOR BREAKFAST, VOLUME 9

BLAZE WARD

KNOTTED ROAD PRESS

Pulp Speed for Professional Writers
Business for Breakfast, Volume 9
Copyright © 2018 Blaze Ward
All rights reserved
Published 2018 by Knotted Road Press
www.KnottedRoadPress.com

ISBN: 978-1-943663-89-7

Disclaimer

This book is provided for general educational purposes. While the author has used her best efforts in preparing this book, Knotted Road Press makes no representation with respect to the accuracy or completeness of the contents, or about the suitability of the information contained herein for any purpose. All content is provided "as is" without warranty of any kind.

Never miss a release!

If you'd like to be notified of new releases, sign up for my newsletter.

I only send out newsletters once a quarter, will never spam you, or use your email for nefarious purposes. You can also unsubscribe at any time.
http://www.BlazeWard.com/newsletter/

ALSO BY BLAZE WARD

The Jessica Keller Chronicles

Auberon

Queen of the Pirates

Last of the Immortals

Goddess of War

Flight of the Blackbird

The Red Admiral

St. Legier

Additional Alexandria Station Stories

The Story Road

Siren

The Science Officer Series

The Science Officer

The Mind Field

The Gilded Cage

The Pleasure Dome

The Doomsday Vault

The Last Flagship

The Hammerfield Gambit

The Hammerfield Payoff

Doyle Iwakuma Stories

The Librarian

Demigod

Greater Than The Gods Intended

Other Science Fiction Stories

Myrmidons

Moonshot

Menelaus

Earthquake Gun

Moscow Gold

Fairchild

White Crane

The Collective Universe

The Shipwrecked Mermaid

Imposters

1

WHAT IS PULP SPEED?

We should start off by talking about this thing called Pulp Speed. This is another term for Really Freaking Fast. To understand the background, we need to go back to the era of the pulp writers, which is generally from the end of the First World War, give or take, up until perhaps the end of the Fifties. So about a long generation of time.

In those days, there were not a lot of books published in the field we know today as science fiction. The modern paperback novel, as we know it, came about after World War Two, as a result of all the books that the US Government printed for soldiers during the war. That taught an entire generation of men (and women) to read for pleasure.

Before that, what you had were the magazines. Things like Amazing Stories, Worlds of Wonder, The Black Mask, Weird Tales, etc. They came and went frequently, with a only few of them surviving long, and fewer have made it clear down even to the present. Each tended to lock into a particular genre, and then tried to generate enough newsstand sales to get a subscription base going that could keep the magazine solvent. It didn't always succeed.

For such magazines, they frequently paid a penny a word (US $) for stories in science fiction. Assuming a short story came in at 5,000 words, the story would earn the author $50. For comparison sake, the median US income in 1940 was $956, or roughly $80/month. Mind you, this is median, so just selling a single story in a month would get you a nice, lower-middle-class lifestyle. And if you sold two, you were living high on the hog.

Not every story would sell, but if you hit once or twice per month, you were set. The key was to write a lot of stories, and send them off. Every story we write is not Pulitzer material. And spending a whole month crafting such a story is no guarantee that it will be any better than one you wrote in an afternoon.

Furthermore, a lot of writers were submitting in those days, and some of them just weren't that good at their craft. The editors had their favorites, people they could rely on to produce good enough work, on theme, on a regular basis, so they could, it turn, fill a whole magazine. But you couldn't publish three stories by Bob Brown in the same magazine this month.

You could, however, publish three stories *written* by Bob Brown, and use pennames on two of them, so "Marc Jones" and "Stan Woods" could also have stories here.

What we had was an ecosystem that favored good writers who could produce good words at speed. They wrote a lot of words. Whole acres of them. Because they treated it like a job.

What does that mean?

These days, you generally go to work and are in an office or in front of a press for eight hours, with a break for lunch and smokes.

The Pulp writers sat down and typed for eight hours.

The new writer, just sitting down and figuring out her craft (and typing on a keyboard, rather than longhanding), will quickly get up to a pace of about 500 words per hour. However, she won't be able to write for eight hours straight.

Writing for that many hours is a skill, as well as a muscle. Treat your writing the same way you would train to run a marathon. Start slow and careful, and slowly push yourself to greater lengths and speeds, rather than trying to do it all at once.

So let's say Suzy writes for a couple of hours, and produces 1,000 words. Then she takes the rest of the week off, but comes back and does it again the next week.

WARNING: LOTS OF MATH AHEAD. PROCEED AT YOUR OWN PERIL.

Let's assume she takes off a week in the winter for vacation, and another week in the summer, like most people tend to do. At the end of one year, Suzi has written 50,000 words.

Let's repeat that, for the people just skimming right now because of the math warning.

50,000 words.

That's a novel. Depending on who you ask for a technical definition, a novel can be as short as 30,000 words. Hugo awards consider a novel to be anything above 40,000 words. 50,000 is a nice step above that.

And all she has put in are a couple of hours a week to write a novel.

So now let's step the math up a little more.

Let's say she writes for an hour every day, five days per week (let's play on the weekends). And we'll take two weeks off every year for vacation. Now Suzy is writing 5,000 words per week.

That adds up to 250,000 words in a year. That's a trilogy of 80,000 word novels. Every year. With me so far?

Now let's go back to the pulp magazines.

These guys (and they were largely men, with some amazing women who had to use male pennames to get published) were writing for up to eight hours per day. So let's call it a sustained 8,000 words per day. Five days per week. Two weeks off.

That comes in at 40,000 words per week. Which is a novel, all by itself, every week. And 2,000,000 words. Two MILLION WORDS PER YEAR.

And a number of folks were doing that. Maybe not to that pace, but they were writing a lot of words.

It came to be known as Pulp Speed. Or writing at the speed of the Pulp Writers. For us, today, the term is measured as something of a slacker's pace. Only **ONE MILLION WORDS** in a year. Because, you know, us moderns are pipsqueaks compared to the giants that came before us, and all that.

So let's do some reverse math. (Hey, I warned you people already.)

One million words, divided by twelve months, is 83,334 words per month. That still looks like a frightening number, so let's chop it down some more.

84,000 words in a month, divided by 30 days in a month, is 2,800 words per day average. I write every day (or probably 19 days in 20, as a rule), but I still think in 30-day cycles. If you only write on weekdays (five days a week), that's generally around 22 days per month, or 3,820 words per day.

So let's write for four hours per day. Or 4,000 words. That's a half day at the keyboard, five days per week, so you've got the afternoon free. (Or you've slept in, fixed a leisurely brunch with mimosas, and started in after that and worked until dinner. Whatever).

Congratulations, you've hit Pulp Speed.

More specifically, what the moderns are calling Pulp Speed One. (For more information, read Dean Wesley Smith's blog, specifically this post: https://www.deanwesleysmith.com/once-more-for-the-new-year-pulp-speed/)

It comes in scales now, since we're all Trekkers in this day and age.

- Pulp Speed One = 1,000,000 words per year.
- Pulp Speed Two = 1,200,000 words per year, or **100,000** words per month.
- Pulp Speed Three = 1,400,000 words (and we go up in 200,000/yr increments from here)
- Etc.

For mathematical insanity, Pulp Speed Eleven is 3,000,000 words in any given year. I know that sounds like an crazy number now, but we'll circle back to it at the end of this book and hopefully by then you'll have a different take.

A word of warning on fast writing. And a bit of a history lesson.

The Pulp writers from the pulp era had an interesting time adapting to the era of so-called modern publishing. The big houses wanted novels, and wanted to publish an author every year in the same week. That got the readers accustomed to looking for the latest from their favorite, the same time each year.

When you are generating a novel every two weeks, rather than every year, the publishers couldn't absorb that amount of material. For some writers, they just stayed with the magazines as long as they could, and fired off the occasional long manuscript to an agent to shop for novel publication.

The other thing that happened was that a given author might be publishing under a handful (or more) of pennames. This was especially true if you wrote across multiple genres at once. A mystery reader will not generally cross over and read SF. Or romance. SF and Fantasy readers might be a little more flexible, but I know one woman today who is a best-selling author under several different author names, in SF, mystery, etc.

I know of another woman who died in the last decade or so, with over five hundred novels published in her lifetime, just under the pennames that people were able to attribute to her. Can we just say *Wow*?

In the modern (read: Indie) world, I can publish a novel each month. Or more. I don't have gatekeepers in the form of Agents or Publishers telling me that there are limits to what they can distribute. Those rules no longer apply, and I'll talk about the future in a later chapter.

We can write as the speed of the Pulp folks, and just publish on our own, and not wait for the Gatekeepers to keep a boot on our necks.

2

SO HOW THE HELL DO I DO THAT?

Okay, so they wrote fast, and you are still figuring out how they managed so many words, when you can barely get any down on paper. Now I want to address some of what my mentors call "The Myths Of Modern Publishing."

One of the most persistent myths that I see with some writers is the compulsive need to rewrite. As an example, I know a woman who had finished the fifth draft of her novel, and put it up on Createspace, just so she could dropship paper copies to her group of beta readers. From there, she incorporated all their comments and then she went back and produced the sixth draft, which I believe was the one she actually published. Did all that work hone the words and make them better? Absolutely. Was is six times better than the first draft? God I hope not, or that first draft must have been a hunk of utter garbage.

The pulp writers did not edit. They were working on a mechanical typewriter, on paper. Possibly with a sheet of copy paper involved, so they got two copies of the document out, but not necessarily.

When they were done with the story, they dropped it into an envelope and mailed it to a magazine. Period. Maybe they did one quick pass to make sure everything was more or less coherent, but when they got to that stage in their careers, the words just flowed.

Once the story got to the magazine office, the editor's staff would read it onto one of two piles: *Pure Slush* versus *People We Know*. These pulp writers quickly worked their way onto the second pile if they were any good, so they got read quickly and favorably. Additionally, the editor would then correct any mistakes they found, and maybe clean things up if it needed a slightly different ending, and then he published it, sending out a check.

They did not go back to the writer and ask if their corrections were acceptable, any more than the writer agonized over every word before sending the story off. (This was before the electronic universe, and in many cases, before the writer might even have a telephone to call.)

Let me repeat that.

The writer did not agonize over every word. They did not go back and fix things. they were typing on a keyboard, on copy paper, and sending the first draft off.

Let's go back to the other example, of the woman who spent a year revising and rewriting, before putting out a draft for her beta team to comment on, and then repeating that process for years on end. She's a great writer and you can find her in the bookstores. I make more money per year than she does and you cannot walk into any bookstore that I am aware of and find my paper copies. (I'm in a few libraries that I know of.)

If you want to learn to write fast, you have to learn to write clean copy the first time.

It should go without saying that you know English grammar, syntax, and punctuation rules. If you don't, go take a remedial English class at the local community college and stop telling the instructor that you know more than she does, because you were wrong last time, too.

Next step, go buy a computer with the right ergonomics, the ones that work for you. I work on a 17" model, with my Windows Taskbar down the left side rather than across the bottom. The key here is to stop long-handing your work and then typing it up later. That takes at least twice as long to do, and does not make the words twice as good. I speak from experience.

Next, stop revising. Period. You wrote it. Keep it. If its crap, learn to write better the first time.

What I do instead of revising is to write in a burst of speed for a stretch, and then take a break. These are the proverbial smoke breaks, but I go walk around the farm for ten minutes or something, because I don't do tobacco.

After the break, I need to pick up the thread of what I had been writing, so I jump back up to the top of the previous section and read it. At that time, I catch misspelled words, or missing words, or perhaps awkward turns of phrase that sounded better in my head. These I fix, en route to getting back into the flow of words so I can continue.

This takes me about five minutes, and reminds me of the words and plot I had been working on. As a result, when I get to the end of the document, I frequently have a draft that is possibly clean enough to go to my First Reader for review.

I don't edit. I don't chop. I certain don't have to go back remove whole sections that shouldn't have been there in the first place.

I also don't get into the middle of the book and decide that the bad guy elf who is my villain really should have been a dragon in the first place, and that I need to go back and revise the whole first half of the manuscript to fix it.

I'll explain why in a future chapter. Just understand now that when I hit the bottom of the story, it is 98% ready for publication. As an example, I just went back through a novel draft and added in my First Reader's comments, and then did a final pass before sending it off to the copy editor to fix spelling and punctuation. 95,700 words increased to 96,700 in the process. More words here and there to clarify things she needed to understand, probably because it was in my head and never made it to the page.

Time spent in massive rewrites and editing is time not spent writing. Simple as that.

You won't start out writing perfectly clean documents. None of us do. But you better get there in a hurry if you want to write fast. People who tell you that fast writing must mean it sucks are telling me (and you) two things: One, they have drunk the MFA kool-aid that says you can only write one novel per year, and must thus agonize over each word to make it perfect. Two, I bet their first drafts do suck, so they assume that everyone else must as well, and that's why six drafts are necessary to make something readable.

Once you start writing a lot of words, your craft will improve. Or, as one of my mentors always puts it: Write every story better than the last one.

He doesn't edit or rewrite. If it didn't work, it didn't work. You go on, and write the next one.

Ray Bradbury always said: Write a short story every week. You can't write 52 bad ones in a row.

There's power in that understanding.

I am aware that one of the great myths is that you learn better storytelling by rewriting your work than you did by writing it, but that usually tells me that you aren't that good of a story teller to begin with, and should work on that element of your craft.

So how do we do this?

3

SIT DOWN. SHUT UP. WRITE

Someone asked me recently what the secret sauce was to fast writing, since he was writing on the more traditional (50,000 words per year) model and wanted to move up to where I was. In 2016, I wrote 420,000 words, while working full time as a data/BI engineer at a Seattle software company. In 2017, I jumped that to 455,000 words.

In February 2018, I finally was at a point in life where I could walk away from a six-figure-per-year Data Architect/Reporting Designer job and write full time.

This is my story (snicker).

In March, I was just learning what it meant to not get up at 4AM, shower and be gone by 4:30, drive 40 miles into Seattle, and get to work when the parking garage opened at 5. Upstairs, I would sit in the kitchen, eat breakfast and have my first coffee, surf the news and my comics, check social media, and then get to work sometime between 6 and 6:30.

After that, I wrote.

And that was the secret sauce. That was the answer I gave him.

Sit down. Shut up. Write.

Words on a page are nothing more than a measure of hours spent typing. Last year, I was averaging about 40,000 words per month.

I wrote for 90-120 minutes before work, then went to my desk and committed art in a language called t-sql.

In the evenings, I might write some on Mondays and Thursdays.

Tuesdays were gaming with the crew. Wednesdays were reserved for my sweetie. Weekends I would try to write in the mornings, and maybe more during the day, depending on the season.

But I wrote.

If you want to be a writer, that's what you do. Write. If you aren't writing, you aren't a writer.

I'm going to be mean now.

How many television shows do you follow on a weekly basis (if you binge on a whole season at once, count that as one of your shows.)? How many hours, that you are not working for the man, are you staring at a screen watching something entertaining?

I got asked the other day what the last show I watched was. I would have to look it up later, and I might put a footnote in here if I can find it, but I stopped watching it something like six or seven years ago. (NOTE: Huh, turns out the show was *Legend Of The Seeker* when I looked it up just now, and it went off the air in 2010, so eight years.)

My wife, the Fabulous Publisher Babe™ has on average one show, because she follows several, and they tend to just barely overlap, so one starts at the time that the previous one ends. She spends an hour or two in any given week, consuming her show.

On the other end of the scale, I know supposed writers who have several shows that they *have* to follow, and they spend ten or twenty hours per week watching the television. Throw in sports that you watch, by the way, with most of them all running about three hours for a game, regardless of sport. And podcasts, if you listen to those when not doing something productive.

And let us also throw in the endless rabbit hole of social media. I'm on FB, but I try to limit myself to ten or fifteen minutes to keep up with folks and their lives, and then I bounce back off again and turn off the WiFi on my computer. (I'm also on pinterest, but I use that for inspiration, seeing an outfit, or a creature, or a something that speaks to me about a future story, so I save it into the appropriate file and then use it later on. That's a big chunk of where the fashion porn I write comes from, BTW.)

So now add all those numbers and hours up and write that number down on a piece of paper in front of you.

I betcha its bigger than you thought, wasn't it?

Worse, multiply that number by 1,000 and those could have been words you wrote instead.

And yes, while you're watching your show you may be consuming story, refilling the storytelling well. That's important, but honestly ask yourself how many hours you need to refill vs. how many hours you're outputting.

I made a conscious decision, years ago, to focus on other things besides television. Art. Sewing. Model-making. Writing.

These are active crafts. They engage my brain and any hands, and keep me moving forward. And I also get to sell the words I have written, so my very expensive hobbies that I moved away from (Warhammer 40k and Flames of War, for those you who know the terms) got replaced by hobbies that make me money.

And I don't have a day job anymore. I get to write for a living.

I GET to write for a living.

That's the other half of the secret sauce.

I love to write. I get up in the morning and get to go spend hours making shit up. And people pay me for it.

Many writers approach the task as a chore that they must do. Like cleaning up dogshit in the back yard. Seriously.

It you aren't having fun writing, it will show through, and your fans will notice that your work is boring and bland. I'm standing at my computer giggling madly to myself as I type. Even now.

This is so much fun. It is not a job that I must work at. It is a hobby that I get to do for HOURS AND HOURS AND HOURS. And I get paid for it.

Does the world get any better?

Do you enjoy writing? Do you look forward to finishing your breakfast and coffee faster so that you can get to the words *now*? Or do you hate the thought of having to go write?

Guess what?

You won't write. Or you won't finish stories, having petered out in the middle somewhere because you just weren't having any fun. Or you'll have to rip out massive chunks in the middle because you didn't really have any good idea what your characters or story were when you started and went down the wrong path from where you are today.

So let's talk about excuses…

4

BUT I CAN'T WRITE...

Yeah, whatever. Are you really a writer?

In this chapter, we're going to talk about the reasons people who identify as writers might not be writing. Some of them are legitimate. Some of them are just excuses and you need to confront them and understand.

The Life Roll

Shit happens. Seriously. You're rolling along just fine, and shit happens. It might be that you get sick. I know several writers with chronic migraines. When one of those hits, you're down for a day or more and not writing, because there is just no brain there.

(As a side note, both my wife and her semi-sister have identified food triggers that were driving their migraines, and changed their diets to the point that 10-20 per month because 3-4 per year. Still happening, but far less frequently. Another I know is triggered by serious pressure changes caused by certain storm fronts.)

A more insidious life roll is when a spouse or family member gets sick, and the writer becomes the primary caretaker. That is more important than the writing. Elderly and ailing parents is another issue, especially when you and all your siblings have scattered to the four winds, and you end up having to take care of health decisions and eventually the estate.

Another reason you might not be writing much is kids. They are young and need you. Plus, they'll grow up and be gone long before you're ready for it, so you need to spend as much time with them as they want, because eventually they turn into surly teenagers who don't want to talk to you for about a decade, before suddenly they turn into adults. You'll never get this time with them back, so don't waste it.

(As another aside, I know a few writers who work in five minute chunks, when they can put the little ones down for a nap. Later, when they go off to school, you might have more time to work with. Plan well and use it as heavily as you can. But keep the focus on the young'uns.)

My wife reminds me to include the monthly issue for female types. Her period pretty much knocks her on her ass for about a day or so, once a month. Some women have it even worse/longer, so there will be perhaps as much as a week where the brain just isn't going to want to commit words. This happens and there's not much that you can do, except know it is coming, and plan for it. Maybe that's when you just edit, if possible. Maybe you go do pretty watercolors instead. Or maybe you consume story at this time, and this is the only time you have reserved for watching your shows.

Here's one that's harder to quantify, but probably hits an extraordinarily large number of you. Writers are weird, compared to normal people. Not-neuro-typical. You don't think like regular folks do. I have a friend who couldn't write, because she couldn't get her brain to focus correctly. What she did was identify that she could do a hard, twenty-minute sprint, get her words down, then take a break and do other things for a while. Then she came back and wrote in another burst. Her brain is just wired differently from everyone else, but she eventually found a way around it and was able to write.

What is comes down to is **Want**. Do you want this hard enough to give things up? To torture yourself? To do the hard things, like retraining yourself to write for 20 minutes and then stop?

If not, why do you want to be a writer? The hours suck. The chances of you being famous are incredibly slim. And you probably won't make much money doing it.

If your response to that is: *Yeah, and?* Then you are probably one of us.

So let's talk about some of the other things that get in the way of your writing.

I already mentioned television. It really does rot your brain, but more importantly, it kills your career, because you'll be dead eventually and don't get those hours you spent on them back as credit.

It's okay to have a little break from your writing to do other things. I sew and build models, plus I own a small farm that requires work outside every day. But writing is my starting point, and the other things I do when I've finished my writing for the day.

Something I hear people talk about is *Imposter Syndrome*. It is a clinical thing, where a writer doubts their accomplishments and as a persistent fear of being exposed as a fraud. Worse, they don't believe that they deserve what they have achieved.

It's okay to have doubts. We all do, but the point at which they are crippling your work, you need to stop what you are doing and address why you have these doubts. Because it will get between you and success, and stay there.

To write a stupid amount of words, you have to believe that your shit can stack up against anybody working (with the exception of Stephen King and maybe Robert Galbraith when (she) gets rolling, because ain't none of us likely to ever be that good, and that's fine, too). You write good stories, and people want to buy them and give you money.

If you don't believe that, then either they really aren't that good, and you are a legitimate fraud, or you have what we call *family-of-origin issues*.

I know a guy who was New York Times/USA Today best seller making seven figures, whose mother continued to call him up and ask when he was going to go get a real job. I know a woman who writes very successful romance, who kept sabotaging herself because she had always been poor as a child, so she didn't believe it was acceptable for her to be making six figures from the so-called bodice rippers.

These myths can be insidious, right up until you tell your parents to go piss up a rope. Or figure out that you don't have to fail the same way your parents might have. (An old boss used to say "Fail

Originally." It was okay to fail, but find a new way to do it every time, instead repeating the same mistakes.)

If you can't seem to write, or can't write at speed, do you have family-of-origin issues that you haven't addressed? That can make you feel like an imposter, because YOU HAVE LET SOMEONE ELSE DEFINE YOUR SUCCESS AND HAPPINESS.

Fuck 'em. The sign on the wall in the warehouse that is my northstar says: "You are responsible for your own career." And you are. Define your own happiness, and stop being an imposter. Because if you doubt yourself, you will self-sabotage your own career and words, and neither will be as good as they could.

So now, let's talk about the externalities of the writer. Literally.

5

THE HEALTHY WRITER

When we were hunters, gatherer, and outdoorsy, we were skinny and healthy. Moving into the factory didn't really change that, because the men were on their feet all day, lifting heavy stuff and moving it around. The housewives were cooking, cleaning, doing laundry, etc. They walked a lot of steps every single day.

And they didn't drink any corn syrup or artificial sweeteners. Just cane/beet sugar and honey. Go look at pictures of the average person from the Fifties and later, all the way up to the Eighties. Skinny, huh?

Over the last fifty years, we have moved into the office, sitting in front of a computer for eight hours every day. We are not moving. We are not walking. And we are (well, YOU are, don't count me, buddy) not eating all that healthy.

About the time we started putting corn syrup in EVERYTHING (go read an ingredients label, I dare you), we suddenly started developing the first hints of the obesity epidemic that has already consumed the United States and is moving on to the rest of the world.

And Diet Soda, with all sorts of bizarre chemicals, is worse. How many people do you know who are desperately overweight, but only drink diet sodas? Shouldn't all that zero calorie stuff matter?

One day, I got angry. Let's just say that I can think of about five people who have ever seen me rage that white. Just before I completely flipped my shit, I decided it was necessary to reinvent myself instead as someone else rather than go to prison. Long story and you'll have to buy me booze to hear it.

Among the things I did that day was stop drinking soda pop of any kind. It will be five years in about a week, and I have had a root beer float (singular) since then. I quickly lost twenty-five pounds. I haven't exactly kept them off, because I started doing a lot more farm work (digging bar and machete stuff) and put about fifteen pounds of muscle on instead, but the belly's gone.

The lesson here is to eat healthy. And I don't personally consider vegan to be healthy eating, because I honestly don't know any skinny vegans. Do you?

Corn is what we feed cattle and pigs to fatten them up for the slaughter. The Asians of previous generations ate rice and were skinny, but that was because there wasn't usually enough food for everyone to eat as much as they wanted. Once there was, they are quickly catching American's in the round category.

For me, a healthy diet is dead critter and fresh veggies. Steaks (beef, pork, exotics) with perhaps a rub, pan fried or broiled. Fatty cuts, too, like ribeye. I also eat a lot of bacon. The wife and I buy the Ends-And-Pieces Hemplers, because that has the best ingredient list. Cut it up and toss it into the pan. Fry it and eat like bonbons, or over salad.

The other half of dinner is a big salad. We keep a lot of veggies in the fridge. Lots.

Spinach. Kale. Mustard greens. Broccoli. Cauliflower. Carrots. Slaw Mix. Beet Mix. Parsley. Garlic. Red Cabbage. Peppers. Bok-Choy. Cucumbers. Celery.

The salad usually has all of that. Plus nuts, raisins, cranberries, and nutritional yeast. Maybe mix in a little dried coconut flakes as well if I'm feeling frisky

For breakfast, I make up a trough at a time. All the stuff listed above, minus the fruit. Chopped up and tossed into the stir-fry pot. Throw in meat. Usually a pound of ground beef we get from a ranch when we get a quarter of a cow, with lots of fat. Frequently a pound of ground pork from the half pig we get. Maybe a can of cooked chicken, or maybe shrimp, or corned beef.

For spice: mustard sauce, fish sauce, smoked salt, pepper, cayenne, bacon salt, dill, chili powder.

Then olive oil, balsamic vinegar, and red wine vinegar.

Throw a glass of water in, cook on high heat until boiling, then reduce to low heat and simmer/stir for twenty or thirty minutes.

When it cools, pour into a casserole dish and throw it in the fridge covered. Every morning, cut out a square and microwave it hot covered.

I drink my morning coffee with honey (local for my allergies), coconut milk, coconut oil, collagen (got bad joints from football as a kid) and maybe a little vanilla. High fat content, because I have transitioned to burning fat these day.

And I take a men's multivitamin every day.

What's all this about? Getting and staying heathy means eating a healthy diet. Mine's not for everyone, but the list of people for whom it would not be an improvement over what they eat now is extremely short.

You carrying a spare tire around the middle? Pot belly?

So then, let's talk exercise. I got land that I gotta mow regularly. I grow rocks and have slopes, so I use a gas-powered push mower. Plus, it keeps me in better shape than riding.

I get out the machete and clear paths through all the damned blackberry brambles so my wife has places to wander. And I get two big "hooves up" from all the deer, too.

We walk. In the winter, when it's pissing outside, we might drive down to the indoor mall and walk twice around the inside (about 2500 steps total) just to keep the motion.

How much do you walk? Get yourself a fitbit or equivalent doo-hickey, and measure it. If you are squishy, the answer is probably under 300 steps per day. She aims for 6,000 in the winter and 10,000 when the weather is halfway passable.

Are you getting enough exercise?

The answer is probably no.

Are you eating healthy?

Probably no, again. I still get burgers and the occasional pizza. Or totally jones for pasta with a white sauce. But those are occasional treats, and not the regular fair. I prepare my own food most of the time, because I have read the ingredients list. I'm allergic to onions, so there's that, but what they hell are some of these things and why are they included? (Hint: they're cheap filler and you don't care enough to eat any better.)

So why does all this matter? If you aren't healthy, it is going to materially, negatively impact your ability to write day after day, which is what you need, in order to be moving at pulp speeds.

Take care of yourself, so you live to a stupidly-old age and still have your brain when you get there. I have known too many people that got to a retirement age, and had lost their minds, literally. There is some research out there suggesting that things like Alzheimer's Disease and such are at least badly exacerbated by bad diet, if not outright caused by it.

Modern research is also suggesting just how many so-called diseases are actually caused by diet.

You have it in your power to live a healthy life. But you have to want to be healthy enough to actually make those changes. Going back to things like migraines, most of them are caused by chemical issues in the brain, and a lot of those are triggered by your diet.

Take a really critical look at what you eat. If you aren't healthy, look at some of the suggestions from folks and see if maybe those help. I have recommended the Wahls Protocol (https://terrywahls.com/about-the-wahls-protocol/) to a number of people who then went and studied it. My wife almost eliminated her migraines following it and a ketogenic diet combined for a significant period of time, and she still stays close. Others use a modified version of it, but the key is to eat all your damned vegetables, because they really are good for you.

And you are in control of your own damned career. And it will last as long as you are healthy.

How bad do you want it?

6

ERGONOMICS AND PAIN

Okay, so now let's talk about the ergonomics of writing. If you plan to write fast, that is going to involve a lot of hours in a single position, banging furiously away at that keyboard. I'm going to talk about me first, and then you.

I write standing up. My kitchen has a peninsula sticking out that is 36 inches tall, rather than the traditional 30 inches for the normal counter. I discovered that when I place my laptop there, it is at the right height for me to type.

I have a bad back. I do pushups and stretch for core strength and flexibility, but I messed it up pretty bad in high school playing football. In the early Nineties, I bought a kneeling chair, so I was forced to sit upright when I was at a desk.

Sitting in a normal office chair for more than about an hour puts me in such pain that I have to get up. Not copacetic to writing, to be in pain.

After that, I bought a better kneeling chair, with a metal frame, and carried it between jobs for two decades, until I left it at the last office for one of my coworkers to inherit. (I work from home, and don't own a desk. Don't need.)

In my house, I am standing just inside the front door, facing into the kitchen across the counter. My wife found me a wonderful matt to stand on, the kind professional chef keep in the kitchen when they are on their feet all day.

And then I learned to type fast standing up. This is a thing for me, and it may not work for you. Your Mileage May Vary. Get comfortable.

But back to me.

I'm going to be standing for several hours, more or less in place. But I rock back and forth on my hips, to keep the back limber. Twist and bend and whatever while typing, including right now (I'm out at CampCon generating these words, using my StandStand.com device to keep the machine at the right height on a folding table. It is a little after lunch and I started this document after breakfast this morning.)

The keyboard is at the right height for me to type. I do not rest any weight on the machine, except when I need to grab the mouse or touch the keypad. Paying attention to my forearms right now, they are slightly inclined, and hover about an inch over the keyboard as I hove. I generally type with about seven fingers (four left, three right) but can use all ten when I need to. (long story.)

Because I stretch in the shower every morning, I can stand for a long time.

And I take regular breaks to walk somewhere, even if it is only so far as the bathroom, because I have drank a lot of coffee and water today and gotta pee.

The key is movement. But more importantly, I have my ergonomics right.

Most humans hunch over when sitting in an office chair to write. I actually straddle most chairs when seated, like at a restaurant, with my legs to the side and my back straight. And I sit on the chair side and leave my sweetie on the booth side.

How are you sitting when you work?

Shoulders forward and down, or back? Spine straight or hunched? Head up or bent over. I look down, but the head stays back. The shoulders have to keep the arms lifted, so they stay back. The back is upright, so I can breathe.

If it hurts when you type, you are doing it wrong and need to change things.

Period.

Let me repeat that: You should not have pain from sitting and typing. If you do, you are doing it wrong. Stop that.

My guess is the keyboard is too high, relative to the shoulders, and you are resting your weight on your wrists in an awkward way that bends them backwards.

There is a science here. If you hurt, fix it.

You cannot write fast when you are in pain. Trust me, I have a disk that slips every once in a while and my shoulders physically slide to the left about half an inch. Think of a nail passing front to back about four inches above your belly button. That's what it feels like.

Pain bad. Exercise good.

Plus, with all the exercise and healthy eating you are doing, you will be able to write longer before any pain sets in.

But get up and walk around.

My wife uses a program on her computer. (dejal.com/timeout for the Mac, workrave.org for the PC.) Every twenty minutes, it reminds her to take a 30-second break, which usually involved flexing shoulders and back. Every hour, she is supposed to take a ten minute break. Usually, this is a walk around the block.

If you can write for long periods of time, you can generate lots of words.

When we do what we call a writing marathon, the goal is 10,000 words in a day, AND 10,000 steps as well. Working the brain and the butt, as it were.

Find your source of pain and then ask how to limit or eliminate it. Exercise and diet might not handle all your pains completely, but the movement should at least greatly reduce them to the point you can put in an hour or three bashing out words.

Those hours add up, both in terms of novels written as well as wear and tear on your body while committing them.

Take care of yourself.

7

PULP SPEED ONE

We've talked about the math of Pulp Speed One. You need to generate 84,000 words per month. And you will not get there out of the gate.

And that's okay.

This type of writing is a muscle you need to develop over time. The following chapters are going to offer some ideas and methods for building those muscles, on the assumption that if you have made it this far, you're serious enough to do this. If not, please regift this book to someone for whom it might actually help.

Still with me? Good. Let's rock.

First things first, you need to track your word count on a tight frame. In the past, the only number I wanted to know what how close to my target (400,000 per year) I could get. I had a full time job and a life, plus writing.

Since I have transitioned, I did something that is apparently rare.

I sped up.

According to *the experts*, most people slow down for the first six months after they got to full-time. I presume that this is due to things like loss of daily, regimented schedule, too much free time to meander down the rabbit holes of the internet, and suddenly having to take charge of filling your entire day with activities, instead of letting your boss do it.

My secret? I now work for the single most unforgiving boss I have ever had to deal with. Me.

February 24, 2018 was my last day. Boom. Done. Kiss you on both cheeks and bye-bye. March was filled with stuff outside myself, so I really didn't write much faster, because there were so many things that were on the radar.

But in April, I had them done, and could push. I decided to track my monthly word count in addition to my annual pace. In March, the ballpark had been about 50,000 words, instead of the usual 40,000. In April I wrote 75,086 words.

WTF?

Hell, that wasn't all that far from Pulp Speed One, damn it. I could do this!

In May, we did a writing marathon, which is where a group of us rent a house somewhere. In this case, it was off-season Lincoln City, Oregon. Get up in the morning, eat, write, walk, write, walk, etc., sleep. You take food down, already prepared and ready to just reheat. Minimal internet. No television. Minimal talking, except when walking or scheduled during breaks.

In that week, I produced a novel (the first Gareth, which came out August 10, 2018). I started it Sunday morning, before we drove down from Seattle on Monday, I finished it Saturday midday, before we came home Sunday morning. 49,058 words. Because I was both pushing, and trying to hit Pulp Speed, I tracked my daily word count, in addition to monthly and annual. Monday was the five hour drive, plus organizing and unpacking when we got there, so I didn't write hardly any words (not enough to even bother tracking).

Here's what the rest of the week looked like.

- Tuesday: 8,200 words
- Wednesday: 7,500
- Thursday: 9,000
- Friday: 12,006 !?!
- Saturday: 6,500

You'll note that on Friday, I wrote 12,006 words. In one day.

While walking about 10,000 steps at the same time. But even my bad days were over 7,000 words, not counting Saturday because the novel was done.

I ended May 2018 at 120,794 words. We mentioned Pulp Speed Three (1,400,000 words earlier. That works out to 116,667 in a month). I was suddenly at Pulp Speed Three. Holy hells!?!

But I was also focused on building my muscles.

Sit down. Shut up. Write.

Healthy. Ergomomic.

But seriously: All Ahead Crazy.

It's the 23rd of June now, and I'm at just over 112,000 for the month as I write these words. I'll hit Pulp Speed Three today, with a week to go. Each Pulp Speed represents 16,667 words over the one before it, so Pulp Speed Four will be 133,334 words. I'll be there before July. Not sure I can push much past, but I don't need to.

My goal is to sustain Pulp Speed Two indefinitely. 100,000 words every month. That's 3,334 daily. Piece of cake.

So how do you get there?

The same way you get to Carnegie Hall. Practice, practice, practice,

8

BUILDING THE MUSCLES

In this chapter, I'm going to talk about some of the methods people use, when they want to learn to write faster and cleaner. A future chapter will cover the craft of world-building, which has tangential implications to speed.

First, there is the *Pomodoro* model of writing. You start with a kitchen timer that is apparently in the rough shape of a tomato. (Yeah, I got no clue, either. Just talking about what other folks have told me about.)

You set the timer for twenty minutes. Turn off the internet. Close the door. Threaten the spouse and kids with mayhem if they interrupt you.

Now write. Do nothing for the next twenty minutes but write. Generate as many words as you can, without hitting the delete or backspace key any more that absolutely necessary. If you need to, kill the spellcheck and grammar check functions, or just ignore them while writing.

When the alarm sounds, then you can stop, if you choose. Go back and fix any spelling errors you find. Whatever you need.

The key here is focused writing for 20 minutes. At first, you will write slowly, but over time you will learn to generate words faster. I mentioned earlier that you might only start out at maybe 500 words in an hour. That's roughly 170 words before the alarm sounds.

But as you keep doing this, you will get faster. You will begin to hit what we call flow-state, when you know where the story is going, and what comes next, and it all just comes out of backbrain like a firehose.

To date, the best I have done in flow-state was to sustain 2,500 words an hour for about three hours, broken into two chunks with a gap between them (driving from where the wife had been doing PT for an hour, and then getting home and going right back into state).

I can regularly generate 2,000 words in an hour once I get into a story. The beginnings are always slow for me (and probably most people). Similarly, I frequently hit the end and have to take a major break before writing the final denouement of a novel. Maybe the next day. But when I'm in the middle of the big car chase/level monster/space battle, I'll easily hit 2,000/hour and maintain it for a while. (It's now 2pm and I'm 7,800 words into this manuscript today. Today.)

So do those hard, fast sprints when you want to start training yourself to write faster. Over time, you will also write cleaner when you do. Trust me, I write a lot cleaner now than I used to. You will to.

Another method people use to measure and improve is the writing challenge. I'm going to upend the usual suggestion from folks, because I think it is wrong-headed.

They say to do a challenge like writing 20 short stories in 30 days. Lovely, but most people can't do that, so they come out the back feeling like a failure. And most writers do not handle failure with good coping mechanisms.

We really should never associate writing with failure, even accidentally.

My suggestion: Do a 10-story challenge. Note, no days attached. Start writing, and count how many days it takes you to come up with ten new stories. Stop. Repeat. Track the number each time you do a 10-story challenge, and see if you get faster. (Take into account life rolls and shit, and abandon the challenge if one happens.)

You'll have ten new stories to either publish or submit. And like Bradbury reminds us, they won't all be bad.

Every time you do this challenge, hopefully, the stories will end up getting better overall, as you get more comfortable writing more and more. And they will come faster.

Along a related path, I used to not be able to write an entire short story in a day. There was a mental issue that said it had to take two. After I did one of those week marathons, suddenly I could. Yesterday, I finished a novel in the morning (third CS-405, aka **Persephone** for later reference). Then I wrote a story midday (Aliens Love Pancakes, Too). And then I transitioned into the Business for Breakfast book for doing your own genre magazine. In one day.

Wow, I can write a story in a day.

That was what the Pulp writers did. Wrote it, pulled it out of the typewriter, stuffed it into an envelope, and had a smoke and a martini. Or a rye. Whatever.

They did a story in a day and sent it off. The next day, they did another story.

Here's an apocryphal story to help ground you in the work ethic those folks had. I don't know who or what or when, but as the story goes, the guy finished his manuscript at 4:30pm. Then he put another piece of paper in the typewriter and spent the last thirty minutes on the next story, because you work eight hours, right?

Before you hyperventilate any more, let's math.

A short story is likely going to come in around 5,000 words as a nice, round number. Even assuming you are only writing 1,000 word/hour (yes, I said only), that's five hours work. You go to work now for eight.

If you hit flow-state, and sustain 2,000 words/hour, that story is out the door by lunch. Hell, let's write a second one in the afternoon and mail it off as well. Pulp Speed.

That's a shit-ton of words (and an Imperial one, at that. None of this metric stuff).

In the old days, that was enough money coming in, if you just sold two in any month, to be upper-middle-class. One a month, if your spouse worked, was the same. You could support the family decent enough, if you managed sixteen per year, spread out.

And they were possibly writing forty or fifty stories each month.

But the world has changed. Let's talk about what it means today.

9

THE WORLD HAS CHANGED

I looked it up, and mentioned the numbers earlier. In 1940, the median income in the United States was $956. Yes, you read that right. In 2016, that median income per capita was $31,099, with a median household income of $59,039.

Median is a specific term. It means that half of all whatevers are above, and half below. Mean or Average income is significantly higher, because a few people make billions, and everyone else makes far less.

Also, in 1940, and until probably about 1980, give or take, one spouse (usually the husband) could make enough money to support an entire household. The wife stayed home with the kids, baking, cleaning, housekeeping, and being June Cleaver. And you could be happily middle-class on that job. Even blue-collar workers in skilled trades could do that. That built this country.

Since the mid Sixties, inflation has been a bitch. Nowadays, most households have two spouses that work, just to come out a little better. Could you imagine in 2018, trying to support a full household on $31,099? So both spouses work, and end up paying for childcare until the kids get into school, if one of the parents doesn't have a job that lets them work from home at least a significant amount of the time.

So now, let's look at publishing rates. In 1940, you could expect one cent per word for a story, or $50 US income on a 5,000 word story, at a time when $80/month was middle class. Place two and you were living high on the hog. Place sixteen per year and you were making branch-manager-at-the-bank money, while never putting on pants.

Slowly, professional rates crept up, but never kept pace with inflation. Today, the definition of "professional rates" by SFWA (the Science Fiction and Fantasy Writers of America) is that three cents per word qualified until 2003/12/31. In 2018, it is all the way up to six cents per word, which is generally universal, with big magazines starting to pay big name authors as much as ten cents per word.

So let's assume you aren't a major player, but sell a story to a major magazine, and they pay six cents per word. Five thousand words. $300. Yes, you read that right. Three hundred dollars US.

Now, let's look at how few markets there are now for short fiction, compared to the old days. Gardner Dozois, who everyone generally accepts as the expert on all things publishing, listed three major magazines in his 2016 Year's Best Of anthology. There were another twenty or so down a tier, and maybe another fifty or so down a tier from that. But many of those aren't going to be paying professional rates. That's why they tend to be third tier.

You cannot make a living writing short fiction today.

If your spouse worked full time, and you wrote full time, you would need to place one hundred stories into magazines paying professional rates, in a single year, to make $30,000. Think that's going to happen? Hell, if you're that good, they'll be paying you ten cents per word, so you'll only have to place sixty stories. Or one to two every single week of the year. Or five every single month.

And that's just making $30,000/year.

Most of the writers you know are working a day job to pay bills, and writing on the side. That's a significant reason for talking about how to write faster, because you might only have ten hours per week that you can put into writing. You better make them count.

So what can you do to make money?

When you get to writing faster, you can continue to write short fiction, and try to place it in the major magazines. The pros I know refer to that as advertising they get paid for, because someone reads your story and then wants to find more, so they go look you up.

Here is where I will divide the world into three pieces, and then ignore two of them for the most part.

You can send everything in to the major markets, be happy with what sells, and put the rest in a trunk. That's what most writers had to do, until very recently. You wrote it, it didn't sell, so you were done. Maybe if you got famous later, someone would want to come back and publish a collection of your early work as a way to cash in.

In the early part of this century, Jeff Bezos (CEO of Amazon, Inc.) changed the future. He made it possible, and even easy, for people to publish themselves. In the past, you might pay some company to publish your book for you. This was the vanity press, which is still a term many of the old dinosaurs use to describe those of us who are Indie writers. (And why I won't ever work with a few of them.)

Now, anybody could decide to publish their own work on Amazon, and anyone could buy it. No more gatekeepers. Agents and Publishers these days decide who is good enough to be in print in Traditional Publishing (read: New York City). Jeff took that power away from them.

As what we call a **Hybrid** writer, you can send those stories off to the major markets to see if they will sell. If they don't, you can put them up yourself, as an Indie. (If you choose to only sell through **TradPub**, you sent it off and trunked it when it didn't.)

For the Hybrid, they get paid for their story, and the magazine is a way for readers to discover them. The follow-up is that they put everything else up on places like Amazon, iTunes, Kobo, etc., and people can buy them directly, paying you most of the money.

I am an **Indie**. At present (summer 2018), I have never had a professional sale, as they count such things. Last year, I experienced enough of a sales surge that I could contemplate walking away from having any job at all, beyond full-time writer. My writing income alone was more than that household number I quoted above, and then I had a six-figure data nerd job on top of that. Life was good.

I don't even bother sending my fiction off to the markets. (One notable exception is when I write a *Hive* story, because the New Yorker has the best and fastest rejection policy in the world. And I've come close to selling to them.) Some of those markets will sit on your story for a year or two before they reject or accept it. Sometime longer. I'd lose track, writing at this speed, even with a spreadsheet.

Instead, I publish them directly and let my fans buy them. Better, I can take sets of the short stuff and bundle it up into collections under the brand name of "Beyond the Mirror." And I can do themes or collections on characters, when have enough with a single group. (Coming soon, in a few instances.)

But seriously, for me the money is not in short fiction. Even Indie.

If you charge less than $2.99 for your story, Amazon's royalty to you is 30%. So if I sell a story on Jeff's site for $0.99, I get paid about $0.29 every time it sells. From $2.99 to $9.99, I get 70%. So my Jessica Keller books at $5.99 earns me about $4.17, after delivery fees. Above $9.99, the rate drops to 30% again, so we need to keep them in the sweet spot.

And fans will get enraged if they feel you are overcharging them. So I sell my Science Officer novellas (24,000-32,000 words) for $2.99, and my longer novels for $5.99, with stops in between for shorter novels.

You can make a nice living, putting out lots of fiction on the major distributors, without ever going through the magazines or New York. I am doing so.

So my suggestion to you is this: When you start to write faster and faster, you should consider writing novels. Further, you should write trilogies, series, and extended universe work, which I will explain shortly.

10

THE BIGGER PICTURE

Readers have gotten trained by really good television to expect long arcs of stories. Things that run across entire seasons or BBC series. In the old days, a novelist could get away with just writing lots of singular novels, but readers like to spend time with favorite characters, so there is money to be made. How many Scarlet Pimpernel books were there, by the time she finished? Or Zorro? You should look that answer up, just to be rudely surprised that nothing has really changed. And those were a century ago.

You can make money with individual novels, but I recommend you consider the trilogy at the bottom end, and the extended universe at the top.

What the hell is he talking about?

A **trilogy** is a three-book set, that generally tells the three individual stories over the course of a longer arc, where each book itself is an Act of the larger one.

A **series** is longer. My Jessica Keller novels will wrap up after nine or ten volumes (it depends on how Eight goes, which I will start later in the summer). My Science Officer books had eight novellas in Season One alone. I have a short story collection that is number nine, and then I will start Season Two and probably have eight more stories. I'm guessing the series will end after seventeen novellas, but I might go longer.

Extended universe is what happens when you write lots of

different stories set into the same world, with overlap. The Science Officer and Jessica Keller are an example, with six thousand years separating them, but Suvi showing up in both places. Throw in Lansdowne, Doyle Iwakuma, Henri Baudin, Handsome Robb, and John-Pierre, and I have stories spanning eight thousand years of human history, but all tied to the same universe. At this moment, that is over twenty stories, most of them novella or longer.

And I ain't done.

But they aren't the same character. They are arcs in and of themselves.

So let's look at the big picture.

You want to write at Pulp Speed One. Many of the Pulp Writers just generated story after story, usually unrelated, while hitting word count. The most famous of the Pulp Writers (in my mind) is Lester Dent, who among other things is known for the Doc Savage books.

One of the advantages of the Long Model (trilogy, series, extended) is that you don't have to spend as much time on your world-building. I already know Jessica Keller and her crew, and where the Eighth story is supposed to go, so I can literally just sit down one day and start putting words to paper. I have already done the research. (My Jessica bible is 173 pages long right now, and 27,182 words, with two subsidiary documents that I only need when writing Imperial Land Forces and the Grand Army of the Republic.)

I highly recommend having a series bible before you start writing. Or the moment you realize that this is a series and you will be revisiting these characters. For me, the bible contains every character description. Every ship. Every planet. Notes on cultures and currencies. The works. Anything I need to look up later goes in.

This means I don't have to waste time cracking open an old manuscript and dinking around until I find the thing I had forgotten, like what color eyes Denis Jež has. Because I don't remember shit like that. (Jessica's are green, because I need that at my fingertips.)

Writing fast means organizing yourself as much as you possibly can. Every minute spent looking something up is at least three minutes you aren't writing. (And the joy of grand, epic space opera is that I cannot be wrong with my technology. I can only be inconsistent.)

You want to write fast. The less time you have to spend world-building during or between projects, the better off you will be.

Pulp Speed One means 84,000 words, month over month. If you just wrote 40,000 word novels, that's two of them every month. Are you paying attention? You'll write a trilogy in six weeks.

I like to joke with my wife that I took a five novel break after writing the seventh Jessica Keller novel. Those five novels occurred in about ten weeks. And they represent the first two Star Dragon novels (new series I'm expecting to run at least six eventually) and the complete CS-405 trilogy (self-contained trilogy, that is extended from Jessica Keller and follows immediately after Book Seven.).

I'm writing at Pulp Speed Three, and I might hit Pulp Speed Four in June. (It is now 3:30 PM, and I'm 10,000 words into this manuscript today. TODAY. I'm about thirty minutes from 116,667 for the month, on the 23rd. You can do this, too.)

So think about how you can write many stories about the same general set of characters. It will speed you up at a time when you want to write faster. And it will please your fans, because they can become emotionally involved with something huge that the two of you can return to for years and years of excitement and profit.

11

ALL AHEAD CRAZY

I talked about this in a recent blog post that became the genesis for this book. But I'm in the middle of the backcountry with a generator and a laptop, and no interwebs, so I can't look it up right now, and won't fix it later if I miss some things.

- *Pulp Speed One = 1,000,000/yr*
- Pulp Speed Two = 1,200,000/yr
- Three = 1,400,000
- Four = 1,600,000
- Five = 1,800,000
- **Six = 2,000,000**
- Seven = 2,200,000
- Eight = 2,400,000
- Nine = 2,600,000
- Ten = 2,800,000
- **Eleven = 3,000,000**

I was writing 40,000 words per month, give or take. Then I got close enough to Pulp Speed One, once I started tracking my monthly numbers, to inspire me to push a little harder.

In May and June I had writing marathons that skew my numbers:

a week in Lincoln City, and four days at CampCon (where I am right now).

But let's talk crazy. Really crazy.

Two Million words per year crazy.

Pulp Speed Six averages out at 166,667 words per month, sustained.

I write pretty much every day these days, because OMG. I get to go write.

So 166,667 divided by 30 equals 5,556 words per day.

If this is my job, then I'm supposed to have my ass at the keyboard for eight hours writing. If I'm on pace, that is supposed to average out at 8,000 words per day. So let's assume I'm only going to work five days per week, instead of seven. That's 7,576 words, each of those five days. I'm still supposed to be writing 8,000 per day, so why the hell can't I aspire to Pulp Speed Six, once I get my brain muscles stronger?

Now, let's get frightening. Let's assume I get to a point in my writing where I can hit flow-state and sustain it for long stretches. Two options: First, I only write four to five hours per day, and generate those 8,000 words I need to maintain my crazy pace. Two: I hit and hold flow-state for long stretches.

I mentioned earlier that when I was at Lincoln City, I hit 12,006 words one of the days I was writing.

Pulp Speed Eleven is THREE MILLION WORDS per year.

Five days per week. Fifty weeks per year. That only requires me to write twelve thousand words per day. Less if I write six days per week, or, heaven forbid, seven. Or write through without really taking two weeks of vacation.

I've written twelve thousand words in a day. And it was part of a larger sequence where I kept going. Hell, I'm at eleven thousand right now on this manuscript you are reading. The one I started after breakfast this morning.

TWELVE THOUSAND WORDS PER DAY.

Holy shitballs, batman!

But think about it. Let's hit flow state off and on all day. Let's drag our ass out of bed kinda early in the morning and blast through breakfast, because *OMG I GET TO GO WRITE!!!* Now, let's work maybe a little later than the 5pm whistle. At the marathon, that's exactly what I did, and I was still learning how to write faster than what I have been doing. As I remember it, I actually looked up at one point, mid-week, and announced "I've just hit Pulp Speed One" and it was the middle of May. I got to 120,794 words in May.

And there was much rejoicing.

There is no reason you cannot do the same thing. You can achieve *All Ahead Crazy*.

But you have to want it. You have to have a most perverse work ethic, because there is no time for goofing off, or social media, or whatever. This is supposed to be a job.

If you work for yourself, you will drive yourself as hard as you want to.

I expect that there will be days where I write for a few hours and just don't have it in me. It happens. Better to recognize it and stop, rather than write really bad words that you have to go back and undo later.

There will be days where I hit crazy speeds. I only want to maintain Pulp Speed Two or Three, because I still have to do editing work on stories, after I get them back from my first readers.

Yeah, **only** Pulp Speed Two or Three. Only 100,000-120,000 words per month. Nothing, right?

Holy shitballs, captain, we can do this.

So let's talk about flow-state and speed.

12

THE RUNNER'S HIGH

When a distance runner gets into the zone in their head, and holds it, there is this tremendous high for them. Adrenaline and all the happy chemicals dump magical thoughts into their heads. You will feel it, too.

In flow-state, you achieve what the martial arts masters frequently call No-Mind. There is no you there. You simply become the written word. I tell people that at that speed I'm not thinking, I'm only taking dictation.

Backbrain has all the words, and it sending them out through the fingers without frontbrain being involved. That's what happens when you get going at All Ahead Crazy and maintain your pace for hours and hours. Runner's High.

It is not better than sex, but you can see it from there, which is saying something.

You will not, however, achieve it overnight. I didn't.

I've worked my ass off for several years, committing myself to the craft of writing fast with quality. Carving out time to do my own one hour sprints every morning before work, because that might be the only time I got a chance to write in a day.

I wanted it that bad.

For me, the only way I will achieve my measure of success is to put out an Imperial shit-ton of material that makes my fans happy. And makes me happy.

You cannot do this if you are not having fun, healthy, and pain-free.

You cannot do this if you listen to the Imposter Syndrome.

You cannot do this if you do not **believe**.

After that, though, it is just the time with ass at the keyboard, committing words.

Every distraction that comes along must pass the *WIBBOW* test. It goes like this:

You want me to do something for you?

Maybe.

"Would I Be Better Off Writing?"

WIBBOW

Some projects will be worth taking the time off from writing. I sew when I need to do something creative that is not words. Other projects will not be worth the interruption. How many hours did you spend watching the game? Or marathon-binging on the latest television show? Will it be worth it?

The other test my wife talks about is the Giggle Test. When she has a choice between several *Next Projects*, which one will make her giggle the most?

She is standing next to me at CampCon, writing the first of the new Seattle Trolls trilogy she started this week. We just went for a walk and she was talking about all the silly, light bits and giggles she inserted, while describing a battle where a group of demons commit a xenocide, if I got the details right.

She's giggling as she writes. You were giggling as you read some sections of this book, because I giggled as I wrote them.

Writing must be fun if you are going to commit that much effort to it. Period. You cannot be half-hearted and then dedicate thousands of hours per year at it.

For most of you, the day-job is frequently described as soul-sucking, depending on where you work. But you can escape it by coming home and writing, or whatever art it is that you want to commit. But it must be something that you are absolutely loving to do.

You must get up in the morning and think to yourself: OMG I GET TO GO WRITE NOW!!!

Anything less, and you will burn yourself out and begin to utterly hate writing. Do not make this commitment unless you are ready to walk down that road.

Decades ago, I studied a Vietnamese form of Kung-fu, when I lived in LA and drove down to Garden Grove to the dojo. Frequently, I was the ONLY white person in the room. The Master would speak to the class for five minutes or more in Vietnamese, which I don't speak. (He only had about two hundred words of English, even in the early Nineties.) At the end of those five minutes, I might get a two or three sentence meta-translation. "He was talking about X" kind of thing.

I learned the art by watching that man move. By understanding how he had to do something physically in order to end up where he was. I have a background in dance and physicality, so I understand the body well enough to do that.

The first degree they award is black, and it goes up from there, but I got to a second degree before I ended up moving out of SoCal. (And decided not to take them up on the offer of free board, if I wanted to live and study at a Buddhist monastery in Houston, but that's another story.)

I had to commit to doing this thing. And finding my own way to the top of the mountain, because everybody else could follow the map that was ritten in Vietnamese, and I had to walk through the jungle itself to find it.

But I found my joy there. I miss it, today, but I'm glad I did it.

You must find the joy in your art before you can step up and write at crazy speeds. Hopefully, some of my advice in here will be helpful in unlocking the things you need to do this.

First, find happiness.

Then Health.

And then the words will flow, just as fast as you want them to.

shade and sweet water,

BD

(normally) West of The Mountains, WA

[4:30 pm, day one, 12,157 words, and 8441 steps. Dinner to follow]

Ps. After dinner, started writing Summer Witch, *and added another*

2210 words. Ended the day at 14,400 words and 12,000 steps. It is possible.

    All Ahead Crazy

13

APPENDIX: HEINLEIN'S RULES FOR WRITERS

Dean Wesley Smith has a wonderful book on Heinlein's Rules for Writers (https://www.deanwesleysmith.com/heinleins-rules-introduction/), and why they matter so much. I highly recommend his book to help you achieve some of the crazy speeds.

WITHOUT EXPLANATION

1. You must write.
2. You must finish what you start.
3. You must refrain from rewriting except to editorial order.
4. You must put it on the market.
5. You must keep it on the market until sold.

READ MORE!

Be sure to pick up the other books in the Business for Breakfast series!

The Beginning Professional Writer
The Beginning Professional Publisher
The Beginning Professional Storyteller
The Intermediate Professional Storyteller
Business Planning for Professional Publishers
The Healthier Professional Writer
The Three Act Structure for Professional Writers
How to Launch a Magazine for Professional Publishers
Pulp Speed for the Professional Writer
Growing your Professional Artist

ABOUT THE AUTHOR

Blaze Ward writes science fiction in the Alexandria Station universe: The Jessica Keller Chronicles, The Science Officer series, The Doyle Iwakuma Stories, and others. He also writes about The Collective as well as The Fairchild Stories and Modern Gods superhero myths. You can find out more at his website www.blazeward.com, as well as Facebook, Goodreads, and other places.

Blaze's works are available as ebooks, paper, and audio, and can be found at a variety of online vendors (Kobo, Amazon, iBooks, and others). His newsletter comes out quarterly, and you can also follow his blog on his website. He really enjoys interacting with fans, and looks forward to any and all questions-even ones about his books!

Never miss a release!

If you'd like to be notified of new releases, sign up for my newsletter.

I only send out newsletters once a quarter, will never spam you, or use your email for nefarious purposes. You can also unsubscribe at any time.

http://www.blazeward.com/newsletter/

ABOUT KNOTTED ROAD PRESS

Knotted Road Press fiction specializes in dynamic writing set in mysterious, exotic locations.

Knotted Road Press non-fiction publishes autobiographies, business books, cookbooks, and how-to books with unique voices.

Knotted Road Press creates DRM-free ebooks as well as high-quality print books for readers around the world.

With authors in a variety of genres including literary, poetry, mystery, fantasy, and science fiction, Knotted Road Press has something for everyone.

Knotted Road Press
www.KnottedRoadPress.com